Includes Five SAT Words to Know
MEETS STATE AND NATIONAL STANDARDS
South America
A Continent of Countries of Amazing Proportions!
IT'S YOUR WORLD
LIVE WORK PLAY LEARN
Where Do You Want to Go?
TIME ZONE • CULTURE • CUSTOMS • CLOTHING • HISTORY
FOOD • CULTURE • CUSTOMS • CLOTHING • HISTORY • LANDMARKS
Hey! It's Easter Island! Do you want to go?
By Carole Marsh

Live • Work • Play • Learn

GALLOPADE INTERNATIONAL

Gallopade International is introducing SAT words that kids need to know in our books. The SAT words in this book have a gray box around them. Students can look up the definitions and increase their vocabulary. Happy Learning!

Gallopade is proud to be a member and supporter of these educational organizations and associations:

Association for the Study of African American Life and History
National Alliance of Black School Educators
American Booksellers Association
American Library Association
International Reading Association
National Association for Gifted Children
The National School Supply and Equipment Association
The National Council for the Social Studies
Museum Store Association
Association of Partners for Public Lands
Association of Booksellers for Children

At the time of publication, all websites referenced in this document were valid. However, due to the changing nature of the Internet, some addresses may change or the content become less relevant.

It's Your World Books

Africa: A Safari Through Its Amazing Nations!

Australia: The Land Down Under for Mates of All Ages!

Canada: The Maple Leaf Melting Pot Country!

China: A Great Wall Runs Thru It!

Egypt: An Ancient Land of Lore; a Modern Land of Oil and More!

France: The Ooh-La-La Country Everyone Loves!

Germany: The Country of Fairytale Castles and Cutting Edge Science!

Greece: A Volcanic Land of Ancient Olympic Origins!

India: Land of Six Senses and Intriguing Mystery!

Italy: The Country of Amazing Fountains and Awesome Arts!

Japan: An Island Country of Endless Intrigue!

Mexico: A Colorful Land of Exotic Culture!

Middle East: Ancient Countries of Current Events Headlines!

Russia: The Great Bear and Its Dramatic History!

South America: A Continent of Countries of Amazing Proportions!

United Kingdom: The Country of Ships, Sealing Wax, Cabbages, and Kings!

Other Carole Marsh Related Titles:

The Mystery in the Amazon Rainforest

Spanish for Kids

Table of Contents

A Letter from the Author

From the desk of
CAROLE MARSH

Hey kids,

It's your world! It really, really is!
Of course, you already know that, don't you?
You surf the 'net, listen to satellite radio, watch television shows and movies set all around the globe–kids today are much more "worldly" than in the past and that's a good thing!

Now's a great time to learn something about another continent–such as South America. Why? Because one day, you might actually visit there (if you have not already!). You might go to school there–many colleges have ties with international schools around the globe. You might even go on to work in a foreign country!

Many companies have positions in other countries. Companies are "going global" as fast as they can. They have branch offices, manufacturing plants, and customer service centers scattered around the globe!

So, ready or not: YOU are a Citizen of the World! And you'll want to be a good one. How do you do that? You'll find out everything you can about that country, how it's the same, and how it's different from your own country. What language is spoken there? What customs do the people observe? What foods do they enjoy? What do they do for fun? What has happened in this part of the world and what is happening there now? It's fun ... and the more you learn the more you will enjoy whatever global opportunity comes your way!

This book is a good place to start your learning journey–so take advantage of the world– IT'S YOUR WORLD, after all ... and guess what? It's a BIG world, after all!

Happy traveling and learning,

Carole Marsh
Always with passport in hand!

Why Should We Care About South America?

South America is a continent of great importance in the world! It is home to the earth's longest north-south mountain range, the tallest waterfall, and the largest area of tropical rainforest on Earth—the Amazon! In fact, the Amazon rainforest produces so much oxygen that it is known as the "lungs of the earth." With its abundant plant life, this massive rainforest turns carbon dioxide into oxygen in a big way! This oxygen supports life around the world. It is very important that people protect this rainforest environment!

Oil is another important natural resource found in South America. Venezuela is the country in South America with the most oil. Since oil provides fuel for electricity and car engines, it is a very valuable resource indeed!

One day, you might want to visit some South American countries to see the Amazon rainforest for yourself, take a hike through the Andes Mountains, or fish in Lake Titicaca!

Write home about it!
What will your postcard from South America say?

Top Fast South American Facts!

The Moai on Easter Island

Important facts to remember about South America:

- Close to 380 million people live in South America.
- South America is Earth's fourth largest continent.
- South America is home to the largest tropical rainforest in the world.
- South America's highest point is Cerro Aconcagua in the Andes Mountains, Argentina.
- South America's lowest point is the Peninsula Valdes, 150 feet below sea level.
- In addition to twelve countries, South America includes three territories: the Galapagos Islands, French Guiana, and the Falkland Islands.
- Spanish and Portuguese are the two most-spoken languages on the continent.
- The major religions are Roman Catholicism and Protestantism.
- The kind of money used depends on the country. Here are some examples: Argentina (Argentine *peso*), Bolivia (Bolivian *boliviano*), Brazil (Brazilian *real*), and Ecuador (U.S. dollar).

Now, you figure out the rest!

1. South America has many natural ___ ___ ___ ___ ___ ___ ___ ___ ___, among them oil, iron, and copper.
2. The Italian explorer Amerigo Vespucci was the first to suggest that South America was not part of the ___ ___ ___ ___ Indies.
3. Isla de Pascua, part of Chile, is also called Easter ___ ___ ___ ___ ___ ___.
4. The ___ ___ ___ ___ ___ ___ ___ ___ Ocean is east of South America.
5. The Tropic of ___ ___ ___ ___ ___ ___ ___ ___ ___ runs through Chile, Argentina, Paraguay, and Brazil.
6. Brasilia is the capital city of ___ ___ ___ ___ ___ ___.

Where in the World Is South America?

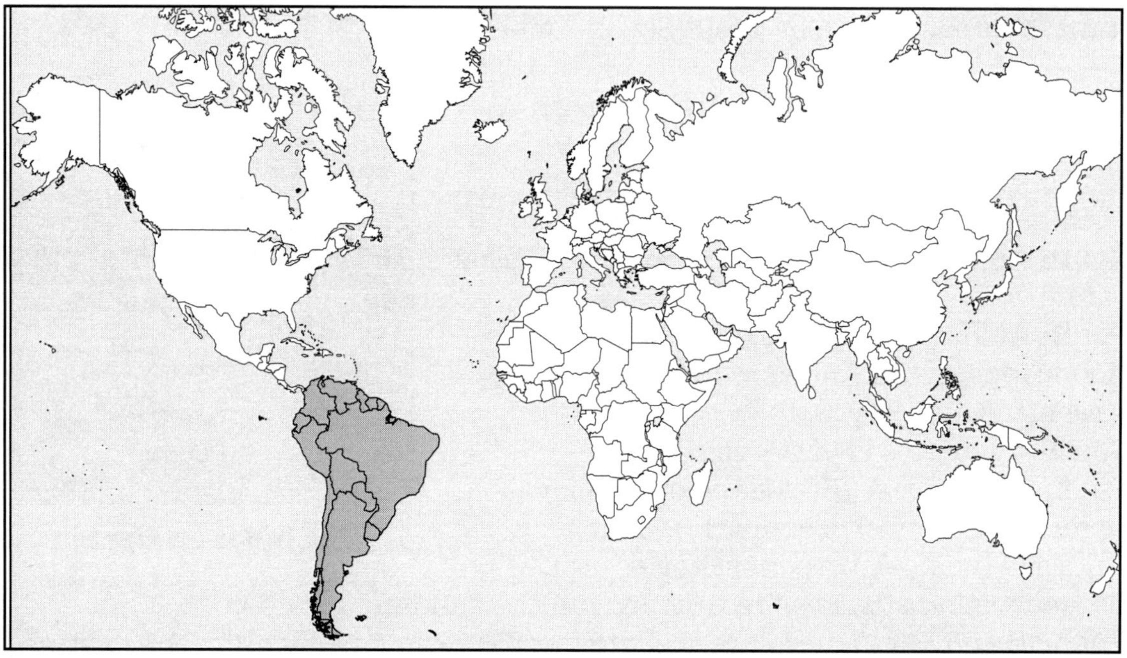

- South America is located in three hemispheres: western (100 percent), southern (most), and northern hemisphere (top).
- South America is made up of twelve countries: Argentina, Bolivia, Brazil, Chile, Colombia, Ecuador, Guyana, Paraguay, Peru, Suriname, Uruguay, and Venezuela.
- Of all the South American countries, only two—Paraguay and Bolivia—are landlocked.
- South America is surrounded by the Atlantic and Pacific Oceans. It only connects to other land at the country of Panama, a small isthmus nation in Central America.
- South America is west of the continent of Africa and south of North America.
- The southern tip of Argentina is close to Antarctica!
- The Amazon River is the largest river in South America. It starts in Peru, runs through Brazil, and empties into the Atlantic Ocean.
- The Andes Mountains span several South American countries, including Argentina, Bolivia, Chile, Colombia, Ecuador, Peru, and Venezuela.
- The climate is wet and rainy in the rainforests, a dry desert in parts of Chile, and cold in the Andes Mountains.

Do You Know?

1. In February, Brazilians celebrate:
a. Carnaval b. Mardi Gras c. Lunar New Year d. Easter

2. Ecuador is a South American country. In Spanish, Ecuador means:
a. equal b. equator c. equestrian

Building Empires!

Exploration of South America caused serious problems for the natives living there. Explorers from Spain and Portugal, searching for gold and treasure, brought a disease called smallpox. Many natives died from it.

Francisco Pizarro, a Spanish explorer, destroyed the Inca Empire after he arrived there in 1532. Around the same time, the Portuguese claimed the area that is now Brazil. Many Spanish and Portuguese settlers moved to the newly conquered lands. They planned to mine for gold and silver and grow sugar.

Growing sugarcane required a huge amount of workers. Because European diseases had killed so many natives, the settlers brought in African slaves to work on the sugarcane plantations. African slavery was very important in the development of South America. Brazil imported more slaves than any other country in the world!

Crosswords!

Use your new knowledge to fill in the crossword puzzle.

Across

4. This country claimed Brazil.
5. Francisco _________ conquered the Inca Empire.
6. South America needed _________ labor.

Down

1. Explorers from Spain and Portugal brought _________.
2. The explorers were searching for _________.
3. Growing _________ can require a large number of workers.

The Amazing History of South America!

South America's exciting history is filled with kings, empires, revolutions, brave explorers, and wars. The first people in South America may have arrived in the New World by crossing a land bridge between Asia and North America. Before the arrival of Spanish explorers, many civilizations flourished. They included the Moche, the Chimu, and the Inca.

Beginning in the 1530s, things began to change! The people of South America were conquered first by Spain and then by Portugal. These conquerors took advantage of the people. They took natural resources from the land and selfishly used those resources for themselves. In addition, the invaders brought European diseases like smallpox and measles. Many natives died from these diseases!

The Spaniards ruled much of South America for many years. Finally, Simón Bolívar and José de San Martín led the natives to freedom in a series of wars for independence between 1804 and 1824.

The 20th century brought modern ways to much of South America. It also brought many problems. The countries benefited from new industries and rich natural resources. But they also suffered from poverty, sickness, and foreign influence. Groups of native South Americans rebelled against what was happening in their countries. Starting in the 1980s, a wave of democracy swept over the continent. Today, democratic rule is widespread in South America.

Timeline!

Number these events in the order that they took place, first to last.

_____Democracy became widespread in South America.

_____South Americans rebelled to gain control of their countries.

_____Modernization occurred in South America.

_____The Moche, Chimu, and Inca civilizations flourished.

_____Spanish and Portuguese explorers conquered the natives.

_____The first inhabitants of South America crossed a land bridge from Asia to North America.

_____European diseases caused the native population to decline.

Famous South American Folks!

Matching!

Match these famous South American folks with their accomplishments.

____ 1. I served as the First Lady of Argentina from 1946 to 1952. I started out as a film actress, but after my husband became president of Argentina, I fought for the rights of women to vote and for the rights of workers. They even made a movie about my life!

____ 2. I was president of Brazil for two terms. I helped to modernize Brazil. Some called me a dictator, but I preferred the title "Father of the Poor."

____ 3. I was a famous Argentine sculptor. I was considered a rebel and a pioneer in the field of art. I just loved to sculpt. Some of my work, such as the *Monument to the Gaucho*, is displayed outside important government buildings!

____ 4. I am a Brazilan architect. I won the 2006 Pritzker Prize for my work. I've been designing since 1954. Next time you're in Brazil, come check out the Estádio Serra Dourada, a football stadium I designed in 1975. It holds 60,000 people!

____ 5. As an Argentine general, I helped secure the independence of southern South America from Spanish rule. I am the national hero of Argentina.

____ 6. I am a Colombian novelist. To my friends, I am known simply as "Gabo." I was awarded the Nobel Prize in literature in 1982! I hope one day you'll read one of my novels. *One Hundred Years of Solitude* (1967) and *Love in the Time of Cholera* (1985) are two of my favorites.

A. Paulo Mendes da Rocha

B. Gabriel García Márquez

C. Eva Perón, or "Evita"

D. Lola Mora

E. Getulio Vargas

F. José de San Martín

Guts and Glory South American Style!

Conquistador

Mixed Up!
Match the paragraph to the word that the paragraph describes.

A. It is an infectious disease that literally means "spotted pimples." It is believed to have been around for at least 3,000 years. European explorers caused an epidemic in South America that killed many people. In 1979, through vaccinations worldwide, the disease was wiped out.

____

B. This was an accounting system used by the Incas. The system used cords of different colors on which knots were tied. The number and position of the knots kept track of goods and resources. The word means "knot" in the native language of the Andes—*Quecha*.

____

C. They were Spanish soldiers and explorers whose goal was to conquer the Americas. Francisco Pizarro led the conquest of the Inca Empire in Peru.

____

D. In this system, the conquistadors were granted the towns and the people whom they conquered. In return, they were expected to protect these people. The practice was abolished after it became clear that the conquered people usually became slaves.

____

E. It is located in Chile and west of the Andes Mountains. It is the driest in the world! It consists of mainly salt basin, sand, and lava flows.

CONQUISTADORS ______

SMALLPOX ______

ATACAMA DESERT ______

ECOMIENDA ______

QUIPU ______

South American Dance with a Flair? The Tango, of Course!

Have you ever watched one of those old movies in which a couple dances with one partner gripping a rose in his or her mouth? If so, then you were probably watching a couple dancing the Tango! This dramatic dance began in Argentina and Uruguay.

It is believed that the Tango was developed with some African influence. It is similar to dances that were performed during ceremonies of former slave peoples. The Tango became popular in Europe and made its way to the United States during the 1920s.

Over time, many regions have adopted the Tango, with each creating its own version of the dance. The original Argentine Tango is a dance of gliding steps that do not follow an exact rhythm. The embrace of the dancers of the Tango is flexible, not rigid, so that each dancer can adjust to the different steps of the dance. In the American ballroom Tango, dancers move with their bodies in close contact, including legs and hips. The Argentine Tango embrace involves close contact with only the upper body.

Elements of the Tango are used in many sports, including gymnastics, figure skating, and synchronized swimming. So the next time you get in the mood to dance, grab a rose and try the Tango!

Draw It!
Get out your colored pencils. Using the information above, draw some Tango dancers.

The Nazca Lines—Mysterious Markings in the Peruvian Desert

Nazca Lines

Did you know there are mysterious lines in the desert in Peru? From ground level, these lines in the sand do not look like anything special. But from an airplane, the lines of exposed white earth stand out like ancient drawings in a secret book. What kind of drawings? There are hundreds of individual shapes, ranging from simple lines to complicated pictures of hummingbirds, spiders, monkeys, sharks, fish, llamas, lizards, and humans. Some are as big as 200 meters across. There is even a 1,000-foot-long pelican!

The forms are so difficult to see from the ground that they were not discovered until the 1930s when they were spotted by people in airplanes searching the desert for water.

So, who made them? Archaeologists believe that the sketches were created by the Nazca culture between 200 B.C.E. and 700 C.E. Why would people who had no means of air travel go to all the trouble of making shapes that can only be seen from high up? That is the mystery! Most people who have studied the lines believe that they served a religious purpose. We'll never really know, will we?!

Word fun!
The Nazca Lines are a mystery! Use the letters from the words Nazca Lines to create as many words with three letters or more as you can.

Nazca Lines

Machu Picchu, A Site to See!

Machu Picchu is known as "The Lost City of the Incas." It is the most visited tourist site in Peru! Built around 1450 during the Inca Empire's most successful time, the city was abandoned when the Spanish invaded South America. The jungle grew around it and hid Machu Picchu from view. In 1911, an American archaeologist discovered the ruins of this once magnificent city. Today, tourists flock to the site to experience its magic first hand!

Machu Picchu means "Old Peak" in the Quechua language.

One of Machu Picchu's primary functions was that of astronomical observatory.

To the Inca, the world and its environment were sacred. "Pachamama," Mother Earth, cared for them, and they in turn were responsible for her care!

The Inca built temples to honor the spirits that resided in the sun, the moon, the earth, mountains, rivers, rocks, trees, and wind.

More than 500,000 people visit Machu Picchu annually.

Create your very own travel pamphlet.
Concentrate on an area that interests you. Perhaps you enjoyed learning about the people, or maybe it was the monuments that interested you. Fold a piece of paper into three sections. This will give you six areas on which to put information.

Be Sure to Be Late!

Customs and culture vary widely from country to country. Sometimes they vary in different regions of the same country. Here are customs and cultural differences observed by the countries that make up South America!

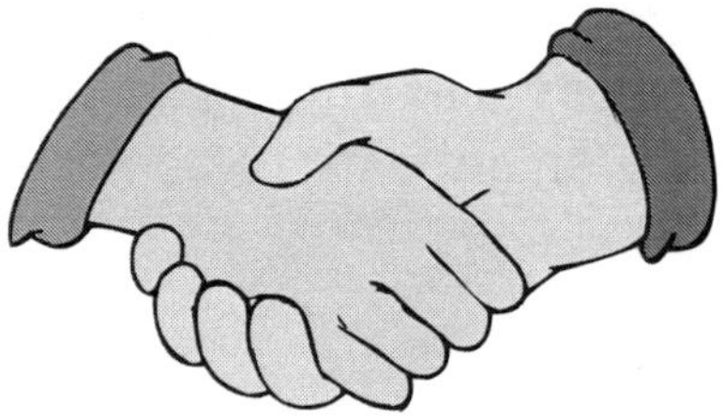

- The handshake is a common greeting in most South American countries. It is usually accompanied by a greeting appropriate to the time of day, such as "buenos noches," which means "good evening."
- The oldest or most important person in a group should be greeted first.
- Guests are not expected to be on time in most South American countries. Arriving 30 to 45 minutes late is considered punctual!
- People from many South American countries hold the fork in the left hand and the knife in the right. You hold them the opposite way!
- First names are reserved for close friends and family. Do not use a person's first name until they ask you to do so.
- Lunch is the biggest meal of the day, and it is common for people to take a short nap, or a siesta, right afterward.

Create your own!

As we have seen, customs and cultural activities can help define who we are. Think about your family and friends and come up with some new customs for everyone to try.

Yellow roses are a sign of contempt in Chile.

Você fala Português?
¿Hablas español?

Two of the languages spoken in South America are Portuguese and Spanish. Both Spanish and Portuguese are romance languages. Spanish nouns are considered either feminine *(la)* or masculine *(el)*.

Match it up!
Below are some common Portuguese and Spanish phrases or words. See if you can match them to the English word.

gato	paper
pai	cat
bebê	pink
escola	father
menino	boy
el papel	baby
el perro	dog
azul	school
rojo	blue
rosa	red

Happy Holidays!

Many holidays and festivals are celebrated in South America. New Year's Day (January 1st), **Easter** week, **Labor Day** (May 1st), **Columbus Day** (October 12th), and **Christmas Day** (December 25th) are celebrated by every country. Each country celebrates its own Independence Day on different days throughout the year.

Carnaval is a big festival held every year before Lent. One of the largest carnavals is held in Rio de Janeiro, Brazil. The celebration lasts for four days. *Entrudo* is a Portuguese tradition of throwing flour and water or eggs at unsuspecting people! Look out! There are parades and dancing in the streets. Samba dance schools compete with each other.

Another important holiday is **All Souls' Day** on November 2nd. It is also known as the Day of the Dead. Because November is actually a spring month in South America, emphasis is placed on agriculture. Rains and flowers return to the earth. Doors are opened to guests who share traditional foods with their hosts. Some of these dishes are favorites of the deceased and are taken to cemeteries. This is not a sad time, but is celebrated joyously with music, food, and prayers.

Write it down!

Pretend you are visiting South America. Write a letter to your best friend. Tell him or her about the carnaval. Did you dance the Samba? Did you participate in *entrudo*?

South America on the Stage and in the Museums

From the passionate music and dances, to its ancient art, South America is deeply rooted in culture. The Tango, "Evita," and the Incan civilization were born in South America.

2.

Notes

1. The music of the South American culture has translated into popular dances like the Tango from Argentina and the Samba from Brazil.

2. Gabriel Garcia Marquez earned a Nobel Prize in literature for his magical realism novel *One Hundred Years of Solitude*.

3. The marimba is the national instrument of Guatemala. It is made of tropical hardwood that creates unique dark tones.

4. Inca artifacts consist of hand-formed pottery, statues and musical instruments.

5. *Evita* was a musical written by Andrew Lloyd Webber based on the life of Evita Perón, first lady of Argentina.

3.

5.

1.

4.

What's for Dinner?

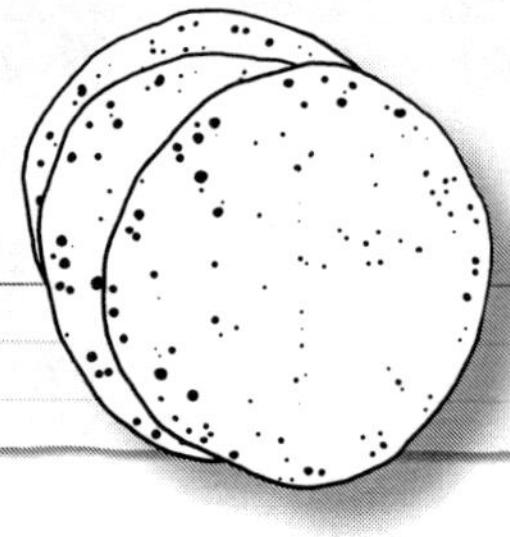

South America boasts a variety of cuisines. Argentina is known for its beef. Brazil combines the cuisine of different cultures. Ecuador enjoys a wide variety of potatoes. There is such a rich cultural heritage that you are sure to eat well when you visit! Take a look at just some of the foods you might find in South America.

Feijoada is the national dish of Brazil. It is a soup made of beef and beans.

Sopa de Maní is a Bolivian peanut soup.

Cachapas are Venezuelan corn pancakes.

RECIPE

Brazil Nut Bread Pudding

Always ask an adult for help when cooking!

INGREDIENTS

4 slices of buttered bread
1/3 cup sliced Brazil nuts
2 eggs
1/2 cup sugar
1/4 teaspoon salt
1 teaspoon vanilla
2 cups milk

mmmmmmm......this was good!

DIRECTIONS

Cut buttered bread into finger-width pieces.
Layer a small buttered baking dish with the bread and the Brazil nuts.
In a small bowl, beat eggs slightly. Add sugar, salt, vanilla, and milk. Mix well.
Pour the egg mixture over the bread and nuts.
Garnish the top with Brazil nuts.
Bake at 325° for 1 hour.

Makes 4 servings

Soccer—A Way of Life in South America

Soccer, or *futbol* or *futebol*, is the grand passion of South America. Whether it involves just a kid kicking around a soccer ball in a field or a world-championship match, South Americans love all aspects of the game. In fact, the first World Cup Soccer game was played in Uruguay, a South American country.

Soccer is a relatively simple game. It requires a goal, a ball, and enough room to play the game. England is considered to be the birthplace of soccer as we know it today. Soccer first arrived in South America through British contact.

American kids play many sports, like baseball, basketball, and football. Kids growing up in South America play only soccer and watch only soccer on television. Even as adults, South Americans continue to watch and talk about soccer. Soccer to a South American is more than a sport. It's a part of everyday life!

Fast Fact:
Brazilian soccer player Pelé has been called the greatest footballer of all time.

Figure it out!
Figure out the answers to these questions about South American football.

1. If a football match is made up of two 45 minute halves with a 15 minute half time, how many minutes will a fan be in the stadium for a match? How many hours?

    ____

2. Your favorite soccer team won 8 out of 12 games this season. What percent of the games did they lose?

    ____

The Andes Mountains

The Andes Mountains

How would you like to take a hike through the Andes Mountains, the longest mountain range in the world? The Andes Mountains run through seven South American countries in western South America. Those countries include Argentina, Bolivia, Chile, Colombia, Ecuador, Peru, and Venezuela. The highest peak, Mount Aconcagua, is 6,959 meters tall (that's 22,831 feet!).

The Andes are believed to be between 150 and 200 million years old. They were formed from numerous volcanic eruptions. Some of these volcanoes are still active today. When they erupt, they can cause strong earthquakes and severe landslides.

Many valuable minerals were formed in the Andes Mountains. Gold, silver, tin, and copper are some of the minerals found there.

Word Fun!

List the South American measurements and features in their correct column below.

7,250 kilometers, longest mountain range in the world, Lake Maracaibo, Tierra del Fuego, Mount Aconcagua, 6,959 meters, between 150 and 200 million years old, Andean peaks, volcanoes

Measurements	Features

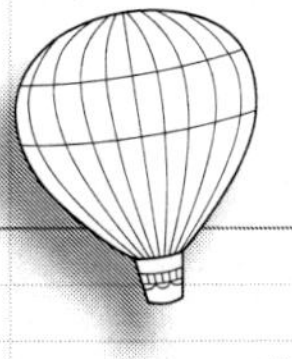

South America Did It First!

Say Cheese!
Antoine Hercule Romuald Florence has been credited with first using the term "photography" in Brazil in 1834.

Dance to the Music!
Andreas Pavel invented the Walkman, the first portable personal stereo player.

Full of Hot Air!
Known as the Father of Aviation in Brazil, Alberto Santos-Dumont designed and flew the first practical dirigible balloons.

Word Fun!

This is fun to do with someone else. Ask a friend for words to substitute for the blanks in the story. Their word substitutions will have a humorous effect when the resulting story is then read aloud.

I want to be the first person to ______________________
(ACTION VERB)

across ______________________! I've been training for this
(COUNTRY)

since ______________. I'm in______________ shape.
(MONTH) (ADJECTIVE)

My ______________________ adventure will begin on
(ADJECTIVE)

______________________. I won't be hard to miss,
(FAVORITE HOLIDAY)

I'll be the one wearing a ______________________
(COLOR)

______________________ and a pair of matching
(ARTICLE OF CLOTHING)

______________________. My faithful friends,
(FOOTWEAR)

______________________ and
(FAMOUS ATHLETE)

______________________, will be there to cheer for me.
(CARTOON CHARACTER)

I'm bringing my ______________________along for good luck.
(NOUN)

I'm confident I'll be the first!

Write It Down!
László Bíró of Argentina invented the modern ballpoint pen.

Space Man!
Ronnie Antoine Nader Bello became the first Ecuadorian to be trained as an astronaut.

Great Defense!
Michelle Bachelet of Chile became the first woman in Latin America to head the Ministry of Defense. She later became the first Chilean woman in history to become president.

The Amazon River— The Largest River in the World!

The Mouth of the Amazon River

Where can you find flesh-eating piranhas, shocking electric eels, and the prey-squeezing Anaconda snake? In the Amazon River, that's where! This amazing river is the largest river in the world! In fact, its basin is the largest in the world and covers 40 percent of South America. The Amazon is responsible for more than 20 percent of all the fresh water emptied into the world's oceans! In fact, the amount of water the Amazon discharges into the Atlantic every day could supply New York City's water needs for nine years! That's incredible!

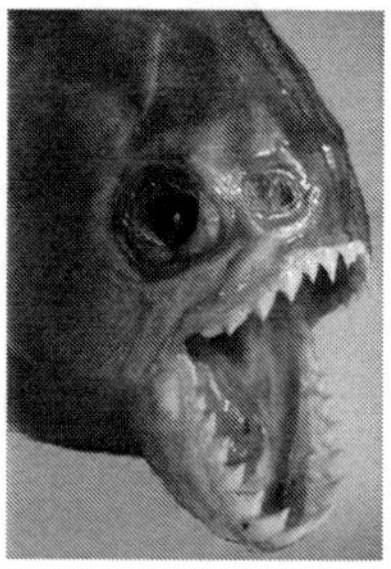

There are no bridges over the Amazon River. Yes, the river is too wide in many areas for a bridge to span it. But the main reason is that the Amazon flows mostly through tropical rainforests, where few cities and roads exist

A simple cross located high on Apachete cliff in Peru marks the start of the Amazon River. Though the Amazon runs mainly through Brazil and Peru, its branches reach into Venezuela, Colombia, Ecuador, and Bolivia. Should you ever decide to take a boat trip on the Amazon, you would pass through mountains, hills, plains, forests, and jungles on your journey! The Amazon is home to more than 3,000 species of fish (including that fierce piranha!) and the famous Amazon River Dolphin called the *boto*.

The Amazon River is a vital natural resource for the entire continent of South America—and the world!

Word Fun!

As you reread the passage above, try to come up with five questions about the Amazon River. You should be able to find the answers in the passage.

Example: How wide can the Amazon basin get during the rainy season?

1. ______________________________?

2. ______________________________?

3. ______________________________?

4. ______________________________?

5. ______________________________?

Angel Falls

Angel Falls

If you've ever seen a waterfall, you know how impressive a sight it is! Angel Falls, the tallest waterfall in the world, is not easy to reach. To experience the falls, you'd have to travel first by air, then river, and finally jungle! The falls lie deep in the rainforest of Venezuela's Canaima National Park.

The falls drop from a tabletop mountain named Auyantepuy. Translated, this means "Devil's Mountain." Angel Falls feeds the Kerep, Churun, and Carrao Rivers below. The original name for the falls is Kerepakupai Merru, meaning "waterfall of the deepest place."

Normally, waterfalls are fed by such sources as river systems, lakes, or even melting snow. Angel Falls seems to get its water partly from cloud condensation! That's one reason why the falls' water flow is not even. Sometimes it is a roaring flow and at other times it is just a dribble.

Angel Falls got its name in 1937. A pilot named Jimmy Angel flew his plane to the falls. He wanted to prove that the falls existed and look for gold there. After landing and admiring the falls (he didn't find any gold), Angel was unable to fly his plane out because one of the plane's wheels was damaged. Jimmy, his wife, and two friends were forced to climb down the high cliffs!

The trek down to civilization took 11 days! News of their adventure quickly spread, and Jimmy Angel had a beautiful landmark named after him!

Revealing Answer!

You're probably wondering what ever happened to Jimmy Angel's monoplane. It stayed atop the mountain for 33 years before it was removed by helicopter, restored, and put on display. Follow the instructions (in order) to reveal where the plane can be found.

1. Cross off any letter "E."
2. Cross off the letter that represents the Roman numerals "10" and "1,000."
3. Cross off the letter that comes before "Z" in the alphabet.
4. Cross off the last letter in each of the three groups.
5. Cross off the third letter from the left.
6. Cross off the first letter in the third group of letters.

ECOXIUYXEDADML EBXYOMXLEIVAERXT FAXEXEIRPOERTMK

____________ ____________ ____________

Hail to the Liberator!

Simón Bolívar

Many South American countries owe their independence to one man—Simón Bolívar! His leadership in the defeat of the Spanish brought independence to present-day Argentina, Colombia, Ecuador, Panama, and Peru.

Bolivar was born in Venezuela in 1783. At that time, Spain ruled much of South America. Bolívar's parents died when he was nine years old. He was raised by his uncle. He traveled to Europe as a young man and came home convinced that Venezuela should free itself from Spanish rule.

In 1810, French forces led by Napoleon Bonaparte invaded Spain. This made Spain weaker. The time was right for rebellions in the South American colonies. During this time, Bolivar began his military career—and what a career it was!

During the rebellion, Bolívar had some major setbacks and was forced to flee his native South America. But Bolívar was no quitter! He simply regrouped and attacked the Spanish again and again. He was quoted as saying, "The art of winning is learned in defeat."

For his efforts, Simón Bolívar was not only nicknamed "El Libertador," but was referred to as the "George Washington of South America." To honor Bolívar, part of Peru split off to form another country and named it after him. Can you guess the name of the country?

Cross it off!

Starting with the first two letters, cross off every two letters to reveal the name of the country named after Simón Bolívar.

Y J B X J O V U L H P I Q S V P K I L D A

____

Ushuaia—the End of the World!

Ushuaia is the southernmost city in the world! Ushuaia means "bay toward the end." It is the capital of the Argentine province of Tierra del Fuego. Ushuaia has a unique landscape made up of mountains, sea, glaciers, and woods. Lumbering, sheep raising, fishing, trapping, and tourism are the city's principal economic activities.

Ushuaia

The Selk'nam Indians were the first inhabitants of Ushuaia some 10,000 years ago. British missionaries came to Urshuaia in 1870. By 1911, the Indians had almost completely disappeared due to death from whooping cough, typhus, and measles. Europeans had introduced these diseases to the native people.

Prisoners built much of the town in the 19th and 20th centuries. At that time, the city was a colony for criminals—locked-up criminals, of course! In fact, the prisoners were housed in a prison where escape was said to be impossible. One of the main construction projects of the prisoners was the Tren del Fin del Mundo railway (End of the World Train).

Did you know?
The lowest (coldest) temperatures in the region are in July and August—that's when the southern hemisphere experiences "winter." Now that's flip-flopped seasons!

Good Points and Bad Points!

Ushuaia must have been a barren place in 1870 when missionaries arrived. List the good points and bad points about living in new, unsettled territory.

Good things	Bad things

South American Fashion– The Panama Hat!

Panama Hat

Do you know how the Panama hat got its name? In the 1800s, these hats were made in Ecuador and shipped through the Panama Canal to stores in other countries. Since the hats were shipped through the Panama Canal, they became known as Panama hats!

The Panama hat is a straw hat with a brim. The hats are woven in a two-part process using the leaves from the toquilla straw plant. The higher the weave count per square inch, the better the quality of the hat. It is said that a truly well-made Panama hat can actually hold water!

It takes three days to weave a basic hat. The finest hats can take up to three months to weave! Panama hats can also be folded for storage without damage. They are popular in warm climates because they are light-colored, lightweight, and they "breathe."

Figure it out!

Help Christina get dressed for her tour of South America. These are some of the clothing styles you could see in South America today. Choose which outfit she'll wear. Color the clothing, and draw a line from the piece of clothing to Christina or cut out the clothing and dress her up!

Assorted Architecture!

Figure it out!
Use the following clues to figure out the name of this ceremonial center in Peru.

- This site was the most sumptuous temple in the Inca Empire.
- This was also the main astronomical observatory for the Incas.
- The walls were lined with huge gold panels which were removed to pay ransom for the captive Inca Atahualpa at the time of the Spanish conquest.
- After it was looted, the polished stones of the temple were used as the foundations of the convent of Santo Domingo.
- The curved wall in the foundations remains undamaged by repeated earthquakes.
- This curved wall is perhaps the greatest example of Inca stonework.

As They Say in South America...

Take a look at these Spanish words. Look familiar? They should! We use them as "English" words all the time!

adobe: bricks made from sun-dried clay or soil
armadillo: an armored mammal, native to South and North America
barracuda: a fierce, tropical marine fish, with fang-like teeth on the bottom jaw
cafeteria: a restaurant where meals are served at a counter and carried to tables on trays
canyon: a gorge surrounded by steep cliff walls, formed naturally by running water
comrade: a friend or companion with similar interests
coyote: a small, wolf-like animal
embargo: a prohibition or ban
fiesta: a festival or party
hurricane: a severe tropical cyclone with wind speeds greater than 74 miles per hour
jaguar: a large, spotted mammal of the cat family; closely related to the leopard
lasso: a long rope with a noose at one end, used to catch cattle and horses
mosquito: a long-legged, flying insect
patio: an outdoor courtyard
piñata: a brightly-colored paper object containing candy/toys that is struck until broken
pronto: a command to move quickly
ranch: a farm on which cattle or other animals are raised and crops are grown
rodeo: a competition of riding broncos or roping calves
savvy: to be in "the know"
siesta: a nap
sombrero: a hat, sometimes wide-brimmed to keep the sun off one's face
tornado: rotating air that can cause massive destruction

Further Resources

Union of South American Nations
http://www.comunidadandina.org
contacto@comunidadandina.org

South American Tourism
http://www.southamericatourism.com/

Interesting Websites

http://www.peru-machu-picchu.com/

http://www.amazonrainforest.org/

http://www.andes.org/

http://www.andesmountainguides.com/

http://www.incaexplorers.com/

Answer Key

Page 7
1. resources 2. West 3. Island 4. Atlantic
5. Capricorn 6. Brazil

Page 8
1. a 2.b

Page 9

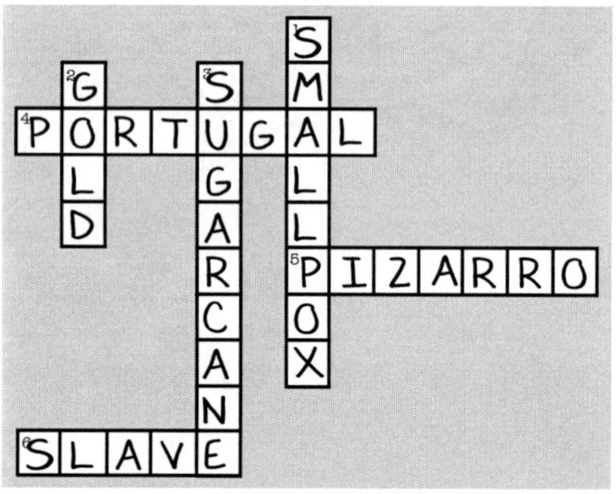

Page 10
8, 7, 6, 2, 3, 5, 1, 4

Page 11
1. c 2. e 3. d 4. a 5. f 6. b

Page 12
Conquistadors – c; Smallpox – a;
Atacama Desert – e; Ecomienda – d; Quipu – b

Page 17

gato	cat
pai	father
bebê	baby
escola	school
menino	boy
papel	paper
perro	dog
azul	blue
rojo	red
rosa	pink

Page 21
1. 105 minutes, 1.75 hours
2. 33%

Page 22
Measurements: 7,250 kilometers, longest mountain range, 6,959 meters, 150-200 million years old
Features: Lake Maracaibo, Tierra del Fuego, Mount Aconcagua, Andean peaks, volcanoes

Page 25
Ciudad Bolivar Airport

Page 26
Bolivia

Page 29
Koricancha Temple and Santo Domingo Convent